This

belongs to

....

Other Red Fox *joke books*

BEST CUB JOKES by Cub Scouts
BEST BROWNIE JOKES by Brownies
SANTA'S CHRISTMAS JOKE BOOK by Katie Wales
THE EVEN SMELLIER SOCKS JOKE BOOK by Karen King
THE MILLENNIUM JOKE BOOK by Sue Mongredien
THE SMELLY SOCKS JOKE BOOK by Susan Abbott
THE SCHOOL RULES JOKE BOOK by Karen King
THE BULLYBUSTER'S JOKE BOOK by John Byrne
THE FISH 'N' CHIPS JOKE BOOK by Ian Rylett
THE GOOD EGG YOLK BOOK by Katie Wales
AMAZING ANIMAL JOKES by John Hegarty

THE FAT CAT JOKE BOOK

Susan Abbott

Illustrated by
Guy Parker-Rees

RED FOX

A Red Fox Book

Published by Random House Children's Books
20 Vauxhall Bridge Road, London SW1V 2SA

A division of The Random House Group Ltd
London Melbourne Sydney Auckland
Johannesburg and agencies throughout the world

Text © Complete Editions 1993
Illustrations © Guy Parker-Rees 1993

First published by Red Fox 1993
This edition 2000

This book is sold subject to the condition that it shall not, by way
of trade or otherwise, be lent, re-sold, hired out, or otherwise circulated
without the publisher's prior consent in any form of binding or cover
other than that in which it is published and without a similar condition
including this condition being imposed on the subsequent purchaser.

The right of John Byrne to be identified as the author and illustrator of this work has been
asserted by him in accordance with the Copyright, Designs and Patents Act, 1988

All rights reserved.

Printed and bound in Great Britain by Cox & Wyman

THE RANDOM HOUSE GROUP Limited Reg. No. 954009

www.randomhouse.co.uk

ISBN 9781862307926

CONTENTS

Tabby or Not Tabby?	7
Show Miaow	14
Squeak Up!	38
Kittens and Mittens	46
Doggone!	50
Posse Cats	54
Lion's Busy	75
Reg It, Reg It	94
Spots Before the Eyes	102
Purr-fection	108

TABBY OR NOT TABBY?

'Tabby or not tabby' is, of course, a striped cat's favourite Shakespearian quotation. Here are some more jokes about our little stripy friends.

Where does a striped cat keep its savings?
In the Tabby National.

If a four-legged creature is a quadruped, and a two-legged creature is a biped, what's a tabby?
A stri-ped.

Why are army sergeants like tabbies?
They both have stripes.

What do you get if you cross a tabby with a sheep?
A striped sweater.

What do you get if you cross a tabby with a kangaroo?
A striped jumper.

What does a tabby wear in bed?
Striped pyjamas, of course.

What's striped and goes round and round?
A tabby in a revolving door.

There were ten tabbies up a tree and one
jumped down; how many were left?
None, they were all copy-cats.

On which side does a tabby have the most
stripes?
The outside.

What's striped and stands at a bus-stop?
A tabby waiting for a bus.

Did you hear about the tabby who stayed up all night trying to work out what happened to the sun when it went down? It finally dawned on him!

Why did the ginger tabby paint out his dark stripes?
So he could hide in a jar of marmalade.

Knock, knock.
Who's there?
Ivor.
Ivor who?
Ivor striped cat at home.

Knock, knock.
Who's there?
Tarzan.
Tarzan who?
Tarzan stripes forever!

What do you get if you cross a penguin with a tabby?
A striped dinner jacket.

Why did the tabby do the backstroke?
Because he'd just eaten and didn't want to swim on a full stomach.

What kind of cat is dangerous?
A tabby with a machine-gun.

What goes in with brown and grey stripes and comes out with brown and blue stripes?
A tabby swimming in January.

What does a tabby suffer from if it has a bad cold?
Cat-arrh.

What's the difference between a tabby and dandruff?
A tabby can have dandruff, but dandruff can't have tabbies.

What does a tabby overlook?
His nose.

What happens if a tabby eats yeast and polish?
It rises and shines.

How does a tabby feel when it's eaten a duck?
Down in the mouth.

What has stripes and purple feet?
A tabby that makes its own wine.

What did the tabby do when it climbed on a diving-board carrying a fish?
A somersault with pike.

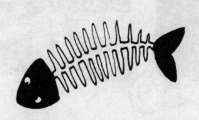

SHOW MIAOW

Did you hear about the man who was learning to steal? When questioned, he replied, 'I've got a cat burglar to show miaow.'

The following jokes will show you how to make a cat laugh!

JENNY: Has your Siamese ever had his eyes checked?
KENNY: No, they've always been blue.

SALLY: Is it correct to say you're going to
water a horse when you give it a drink?
MOTHER: *Yes*.
SALLY: Then I'm going to milk the cat.

What did the scientist get when he crossed
a cat with a gorilla?
An animal that put him *out at night*.

MILLY: My cat's alive with ticks.
TILLY: *Well, don't overwind him*.

What would you do with a Blue Burmese?
Try to cheer it up.

KEN: How big is a cat?
BEN: *What kind of cat?*
KEN: A big one.
BEN: *How big?*

FIRST CAT: You remind me of a fence.
SECOND CAT: *Why?*
FIRST CAT: Because you run around but you
  never get anywhere.

What's a cat's favourite TV programme?
Mews at Ten.

VISITOR: Why is your cat giving me such
  funny looks?
OWNER: It's probably because he wants you
  to get out of his chair.

What's worse than raining cats and dogs?
Hailing taxis!

What's the worst weather for rats and mice?
When it is raining cats and dogs!

What do you get if you cross a cat with a
canary?
Shredded tweet.

CUSTOMER: This loaf's still warm!
BAKER: *That's because the cat's been sitting
on it since it came out of the oven.*

Now you see it, now you don't, now you see
it, now you don't. What is it?
*A black and white cat walking across a zebra
crossing.*

SMART ALEC: What's the difference between a cat's litter tray and a soup bowl?
DUMB DONALD: *I don't know.*
SMART ALEC: I'm not coming to dinner at your house, then!

'Doctor, doctor, I think I'm a cat!'
'Lie down on the couch.'
'I can't, I'm not allowed on the furniture.'

What do you get if you cross a cat and an octagon?
An octopus.

What do you get if you cross a cat with a lemon?
A sourpuss.

A man walked into a police station with a dead cat. 'I found it in my garden this morning,' he said.

The policeman took notes. 'Right,' he said. 'If no one claims it within six months, it's yours.'

What's better than a talking cat?
A spelling bee.

DANNY: Did you hear the story about the cat and the crab?
ANNIE: *Sounds fishy to me.*

MOTHER: Stop pulling the cat's tail.
DENNIS: *It's him that's doing the pulling.*

Where did the cow take the cat when she went to America?
Moo York.

What do you give a bird caught by a cat?
Tweetment.

Knock, knock.
Who's there?
Scold.
Scold who?
Scold outside, please let the cat in.

Why did the cat cross the road?
Because it was tied to the chicken.

What goes clomp, clomp, clomp, squelch?
A cat with wet trainers.

JOHN: What did the cat do with the tellycost?
DON: *What's a tellycost?*
JOHN: Oh, about £100.

Why did the cat work in the bakery?
It kneaded the dough.

What looks like a cat, yet isn't a cat?
A photograph of a cat.

JIMMY: Have you seen the musical *Cats*?
TIMMY: *No. All the cats I've seen are very
unmusical.*

Why did the cat blush when she walked past
the hen coop?
Because she heard fowl language.

Notice in shop window: Lost, black and
white cat by elderly gentleman answering
to the name of Tiddles.

If a cat's nose runs and its feet smell, what's
wrong with it?
It's built upside down.

What kind of cat should you take with you in the desert?
A thirst-aid kit.

Why do cats turn round and round before going to sleep?
Because one good turn deserves another.

What does a cat have when it doesn't feel well?
Gloves on its paws.

Why did the man keep his cat under the bed?
He thought it was a little potty.

What's the difference between a flea-ridden cat and a bored visitor?
One's going to itch; the other's itching to go.

JANE: My cat doesn't eat meat.
WAYNE: *Why not?*
JANE: We don't give him any.

TOM CAT: Will you be my wife one day?
QUEEN CAT: *Not for one hour, you creep!*

HIL: I met a catweigh yesterday.
BILL: *What's a catweigh?*
HIL: Oh, about 8 lbs.

FIRST CAT: What have you done for your fleas?
SECOND CAT: *Nothing.*
FIRST CAT: Why not?
SECOND CAT: *Why should I? They've never done anything for me!*

SILLY SUE: How many times can you take 15 cats away from 151?
CLEVER DICK: *Only once. After that you're not taking them away from 151.*

Knock, knock.
Who's there?
Bernardette.
Bernardette who?
Bernardette the cat's dinner.

UNCLE HARRY: Keep that cat out of your aunt's kitchen.

CHEEKY CHARLIE: *Otherwise I suppose it'll be meat curry for supper tomorrow!*

How can a thin cat put on weight?
By eating plums. With every one it'll gain a stone.

MOTHER CAT: Don't eat your food so quickly.

KITTEN: *But I might lose my appetite unless I do.*

WORRIED OWNER: My cat's just eaten a camera!

VET: *Don't worry, nothing serious will develop.*

A man was playing chess with a cat in a café. Another customer came up to him, watched him for a while, and then said, 'That cat could make you a fortune.'

'Not really,' replied the man. 'You see, he's not that good. I've beaten him in the last four games.'

What's the difference between a cat and a biscuit?
You can dip a biscuit in your tea, but a cat's too big to go in the cup.

GILLIE: How old's your brother?

WILLIE: *A year old.*

GILLIE: A year old? That's the same age as my cat, but she can walk much better than your brother.

WILLIE: *I'm not surprised. She's got twice as many legs.*

HEATHER: I wish I'd enough money to buy a Siamese cat.

HOLLY: *But you don't like cats!*

HEATHER: Oh, I don't want one, I just wish I had enough money to buy one.

Why do Siamese cats have big ears?
Because Noddy won't pay the ransom.

A man driving a shiny new car on an icy morning braked to avoid a cat and skidded into a lamppost. He got out and looked at the car's crumpled front wing, and said sadly, 'That's the way the Mercedes Benz.'

Knock, knock.
Who's there?
Java.
Java who?
Java cat in your house?

What looks just like half a cat?
The other half.

MRS TILLY: Our cat fell out of our bedroom window.

MRS TALLY: *Oh dear, was it hurt?*

MRS TILLY: No, we live in a bungalow.

DENNIS: What would happen if I stole one of those lovely fluffy Persian kittens?
FATHER: *You'd be sent to prison.*
DENNIS: Oh dear. But you'd look after him while I was away, wouldn't you?

POLICEMAN, KNOCKING ON DOOR OF HOUSE: We're after a cat burglar, madam. Have you seen anything suspicious?
LADY OF THE HOUSE: *How do you know it was a cat burglar?*
POLICEMAN: Because it stole a jug of cream.

Little Horace was looking at a stuffed wild cat in a glass case in a museum. 'Mum,' he mused, 'how did they shoot the cat without breaking the glass?'

Why did the cat eat little bits of metal?
It was his staple diet.

Why did the cat eat all the white meat off the chicken?
To make a clean breast of it.

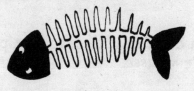

How do cats eat spaghetti?
Like everyone else, they put it in their mouths.

FIRST CAT: Every bone in my body aches.
SECOND CAT: *Be thankful you're not a herring.*

JILL: I'm looking for a cat with one eye called
Freddie.
BILL: *What's his other eye called?*

What's a Scottish cat's favourite pudding?
Chocolate mousse.

FIRST WITCH: There's a strange black cat in the kitchen.
SECOND WITCH: *Oh good, they're lucky.*
FIRST WITCH: This one isn't – he's just run off with the Sunday joint.

HAL: We had to have our cat put down.
VAL: *Was it mad?*
HAL: Well, it wasn't too pleased!

What's the difference between school meals and cat food?
School meals are served on plates, cat food in cats' bowls.

FIRST CAT: Where do fleas go in winter?
SECOND CAT: *Search me!*

A cat climbed a tall tree and then miaowed because it couldn't get down again.
'Why don't you come down the way you went up?' asked its friend.
'I can't, I came up head first.'

How long should a cat's legs be if its body is 30 centimetres long?
Long enough to reach the ground.

The local stately home was holding a garden party, and all the gentry were there in their best clothes. A cat strolled among the guests, and then sat down to wash its back.

'I wish I could bend round far enough to do that,' exclaimed one smartly-dressed lady.

Her companion, the local vicar, turned round to look, and saw the cat busy washing its bottom!

Mary had a little cat –
She also had a bear.
I've often seen her little cat
But I've never seen her bare!

ROGER: Isn't it lucky to have a black cat following you?
ROLAND: *That depends on whether you're a man or a mouse.*

FIRST CAT: I feel I'm going to live a long time.
SECOND CAT: *Well, we're supposed to have nine lives.*

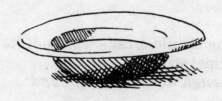

Why did the cat wear pink trainers?
So it could hide in a cherry tree.

PATSY: Our cat is one of breeding.
PADDY: *I know. She's had lots of kittens.*

Why can't a cat ride a bicycle?
Because it can't reach the bell with its paws.

Knock, knock.
Who's there?
Luke.
Luke who?
Luke through the cat flap and see if it's
raining.

Knock, knock.
Who's there?
Diana.
Diana who?
Diana thirst, may I have a saucer of milk,
please?

Which cats have their eyes closest together?
The smallest cats.

What makes a gardener angry?
When a cat plants its paws in his seedbed.

How do you know if a cat's been in your
fridge?
By the hairs on the butter.

SUE: What's your cat called?
PRUE: *Isaiah.*
SUE: Why's he called Isaiah?
PRUE: *Because one eye's 'igher than the other.*

TIM: Our cat's called Ben Hur.
JIM: *That's a funny name for a cat.*
TIM: Yes. He was just called Ben until he had kittens.

How do you start a cat-flea race?
One, two, flea – go!

FAT CAT: You look as though you've lived through a famine.
THIN CAT: *And you look as though you've caused it.*

What does a cat get if it falls in the ocean?
Wet.

What did the cat who had no money say?
'I'm paw.'

What's sweet, has whiskers and floats?
A catameringue.

What's cream and brown, has blue eyes, and leaves everyone standing at the traffic lights?
A turbo-charged Siamese.

Knock, knock.
Who's there?
Shirley.
Shirley who?
Shirley you recognise your own cat?

Six and sixty Siamese pussies sat on seven
and seventy sharp thistles. How many S's
in that?
There aren't any S's in THAT!

What do Siamese cats have that no other
animal in the world has?
Siamese kittens.

ARNIE: Our cat's just like one of the family.
BARNEY: *Really? Which one?*

A cat walked into a café and ordered a cup
of coffee with cream. The proprietor,
thinking the cat would know nothing about
money, charged him £5.

As the cat got up to leave, the proprietor
called out, 'We don't get many cats in here.'

'With coffee at £5 a cup, I'm not surprised,'
replied the cat.

What do you call a cat that's swallowed a duck?
A duck-filled fatty puss.

What did the cat say to the cockroach?
'Stop bugging me.'

Who won when the cat fought a hedgehog?
The hedgehog won on points.

What happened when someone trod on the cat's tail?
They hurt its felines.

What do you call a fat cat who drowns in a river?
A non-slimmer.

Which branch of the armed forces did the Persian cat join?
The Hair Force.

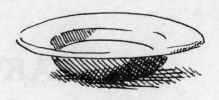

Knock, knock.
Who's there?
Joan.
Joan who?
Joan call the cat in until I've got his supper
ready.

FENELLA: I entered my cat in a competition
and won first prize.
PRUNELLA: *That's terrific!*
FENELLA: Yes, but I wanted my cat to win.

Why do cats paint their paws yellow?
So they can hide upside down in the butter.

Have you ever seen a cat hiding upside down
in the butter? Just shows what a good
disguise it is, doesn't it?

DAVE: Did you put the cat out?
DOUG: *Was it on fire again?*

Which cat should you never play cards with?
A cheetah.

SQUEAK UP!

'Squeak up!' is what you say to someone when you have asked them if they are a man or a mouse. Here are some more mouse to mouse jokes.

FIRST MOUSE: I've trained that scientist at last.
SECOND MOUSE: *How did you do that?*
FIRST MOUSE: Every time I run through the wheel and ring the bell he puts some cheese underneath it.

What did the mouse say when it broke two of its front teeth?
'Hard cheese.'

What's the most difficult thing about
milking a mouse?
Getting the bucket underneath it.

What's grey, has four legs and a trunk?
A mouse going to boarding-school.

What's grey, has four legs and a very big
trunk?
A mouse emigrating.

What do you get if you cross a mouse with
an elephant?
Enormous holes in the skirting-board.

Hickory, dickory, dock,
Two mice ran up the clock.
The clock struck one –
But the other one got away.

Who has large antlers and wears white gloves?
Mickey Moose.

Why did Mickey Mouse want to go on the space shuttle?
He wanted to visit Pluto.

A man who was troubled with mice bought a mousetrap and brought it home, only to discover he had no cheese. So he cut out a picture of a piece of cheese from a magazine and baited the trap with that.

In the morning he went to inspect the trap. The picture of the cheese had gone, and in its place was a picture of a mouse.

What's the biggest mouse in the world?
A hippopotamouse.

What did the giant mouse say as it strode
across the kitchen?
'Here, kitty, kitty, kitty.'

ANNIE: Who wrote 'To a Field Mouse'?
DANNY: *I don't know, but whoever it was I
bet they didn't get a reply!*

What did the cat do when it saw the mouse?
Made a feline for it.

How do you save a drowning mouse?
With mouse to mouse resuscitation.

Did you hear about the young bride who
thought the patter of tiny feet meant mice?

What do angry rodents send to each other
at Yuletide?
Cross-mouse cards.

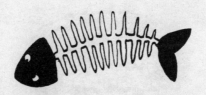

SALLY: What would you do if you were in bed at night and you heard a mouse squeaking in the kitchen?

SUSIE: *I don't know, but I wouldn't get up to oil it!*

A mouse went to a shop that sold musical instruments and asked to buy a mouse organ. The shop assistant was surprised, but he said, 'No one has ever asked for that before today, yet you're the second to ask this afternoon.'

'Ah,' said the mouse thoughtfully, 'that would have been our Monica.'

LARRY: I had a narrow squeak yesterday.

BARRY: *What happened?*

LARRY: I trod on a mouse.

MAN TO PET SHOP ASSISTANT: You said this cat was good for mice, but it's never caught one.

PET SHOP ASSISTANT: *Well, that's good for mice, isn't it?*

What has twelve legs, three tails and can't see?
Three blind mice.

What are furry and go 'eek, eek, eek' when you eat them?
Mice Krispies.

What does a cat with bad breath need?
A mousewash.

CUSTOMER: A mousetrap, please, and please hurry, I have to catch a train.
SHOP ASSISTANT: *We haven't got any that big!*

What did the cat do after it had eaten ten mice?
It burped.

A man had a cat, a mouse and a large Cheddar cheese, and had to ferry them across a stream. If he took them all together, the cat would catch the mouse, and the mouse would eat the cheese. There were similar problems if he took just the cat and the mouse or just the mouse and the cheese at the same time. How did he do it?

First he crossed with the mouse, leaving the cat and the cheese behind. He left the mouse on the far side.

He returned, ferried the cat over, leaving it on the far side and taking the mouse back with him.

He left the mouse on the first side, and rowed the cheese over to the bank where the cat was.

Finally he returned to the first side, picked up the mouse and rowed it over again.

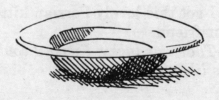

LADY MONEYBAGS: Jeeves, there's a mouse in the east wing.

JEEVES: *Very good, madam. I'll ascertain if the cat is at home.*

KITTENS AND MITTENS

What happened to the cat who swallowed a ball of wool?
She had mittens!

MOTHER CAT: What are you kittens doing?
FIRST KITTEN: *Chasing a mouse round the yard.*
MOTHER CAT: How many times have I told you not to play with your food?

HENRY: I got this lovely Persian kitten for my girlfriend.
HARRY: *That was lucky. I wish I could do swaps like that.*

MARY: What have I got in my hands?
MAUREEN: *Two cats and four kittens.*
MARY: Oh, you peeped!

Why does a mother cat carry her kittens?
Because they can't carry her.

KATIE: What would you do if you found your
kitten was chewing up your favourite
book?
KATHLEEN: *I'd take the words out of his
mouth.*

LITTLE GIRL: I'd like to buy a kitten. How
much are they?
PET SHOP OWNER: *£5 apiece.*
LITTLE GIRL: But I want a *whole* kitten!

A kitten called May was always picking fights with bigger cats. One day she got into a fight with a lion cub. The next day was the first of June. Why?
Because that was the end of May.

MOTHER CAT: Why did you chase that bird?
KITTEN: *For a lark.*

Why was the baby raised on cats' milk?
Because it was a kitten.

SHARON: Our new kitten has a pedigree.
DARREN: *You mean you have papers for it?*
SHARON: Yes, all over the kitchen floor.

How can two kittens born on the same day to the same mother not be twins?
They could be two triplets, quads or quins.

Some children were gathered round a kitten, all talking nineteen to the dozen. Their mother came along and asked what they were doing.

'We're swapping lies,' said Samantha. 'Whoever tells the biggest lie gets the kitten.'

'But that's shocking,' said the mother. 'Why, when I was your age, I wouldn't have dreamt of telling lies.'

'That's it, Mum, you win the kitten!'

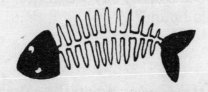

GWEN: I'm going to have a kitten for Christmas!
LEN: *Really? We always have a turkey.*

FIRST KITTEN: Have you seen our new brothers? The stork brought them.
SECOND KITTEN: *They look more as if a seagull had dropped them!*

FIRST KITTEN: I weighed only half an ounce at birth.
SECOND KITTEN: *Gosh, did you live?*
FIRST KITTEN: Live? You should see me now!

DOGGONE!

Why did the cat chase the dog?
Doggone if I know!

What did the cowboy say when the mountain lion ate his hound?
'Doggone.'

What did the dog say when the cat scratched it?
Nothing, dogs can't talk!

If a dog sleeps in a kennel, does a cat sleep in a cattle?

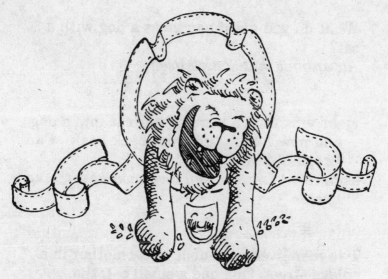

A man once appeared at a music hall with a unique act. He had a dog which played the piano while a cat sang, and the performance was so astonishing that at the end of it a theatrical agent who was in the audience rushed up to him and said, 'That was incredible! I'd like to sign you up for the London Palladium!'

'Well, I don't know about that,' said the man. 'It's not that good, really.'

'But it is,' insisted the agent. 'It's unique. I've never heard of a dog playing the piano while a cat sang. Don't you want to appear at the Palladium?'

The man looked a bit uncomfortable. 'Well, to be honest with you, the act's a bit of a cheat really. You see, the cat can't sing. The dog's a ventriloquist.'

51

What do you get if you cross a dog with a cat?
An animal that chases itself.

FIRST WITCH: I've turned your cat into a dog and now I can't turn him back again. Can I replace him for you?
SECOND WITCH: *Are you any good at catching mice?*

Two men lived next-door to each other in a village street. One had a small cat, the other a huge Rottweiler. One day the man with the cat knocked on the other's door and said, 'I'm very sorry, but my cat's killed your dog.'

'How on earth could your little cat kill my big dog?' asked the neighbour.

'Well, I'm afraid she stuck in his throat and choked him to death,' replied the man.

What kind of fish do dogs chase?
Catfish.

BENNY: Have you ever seen a catfish?
LENNY: *Yes.*
BENNY: How did it hold the rod?

PUPPY: My mother says I'm too fat.
KITTEN: *My mother says I'm too thin.*
PUPPY: How's that?
KITTEN: *She says she can see right through me.*

Why do dogs and cats eat raw meat?
They can't cook.

POSSE CATS

What were a sheriff's cats called in the Wild West?
Posse cats, of course!

FIRST COWBOY: My cat's ill. Can you recommend a good animal doctor?
SECOND COWBOY: *Sorry, all the doctors I know are people.*

What animal would a cat like to be on a cold January day in the Rocky Mountains?
A little otter.

COWBOYS' COOK: I made a lovely stew for you boys, but the cat's eaten it.
COWBOY: *Don't worry, there are plenty of cats round here, we'll soon find another one.*

FIRST CAT: What a storm there was last night! Did you hear it?
SECOND CAT: *Yes.*
THIRD CAT: Then why didn't you wake me up? You know I can't sleep through a thunderstorm!

What kind of tickle doesn't make a cat laugh?
A tickle in its throat.

How does a cat cross a road?
It uses a purrdestrian crossing.

DAVE: A black and white cat crossed my path this morning.
MAEVE: *Oh yes?*
DAVE: Mmm. Since then my luck's been very patchy.

PATIENT: I keep thinking I'm a cat.
DOCTOR: *How long has this been going on?*
PATIENT: Ever since I was a kitten.

What tree can't a cat climb?
A laboratory.

FIRST CAT: I don't like that tree.
SECOND CAT: *Why not?*
FIRST CAT: Because it's a dogwood.
SECOND CAT: *How can you tell?*
FIRST CAT: By its bark.

Who did the vampire cat marry?
The girl cat necks door.

How do you stop a tom-cat smelling?
Put a clothes-peg on his nose.

FIRST CAT: Why are you scratching yourself?
SECOND CAT: *Because no one else knows where I itch.*

Why did the cat sleep under the car?
Because it wanted to wake up oily in the morning.

When can a cat travel underwater?
When it's in a submarine.

What's the best way to catch a cat?
Call out 'Tiddles' and make a noise like a tin-opener.

Why is a cat learning to sing like someone opening a tin of sardines?
They both have trouble with the key.

Sign on newly-planted flower-bed: Cats beware – vicious gardener.

Knock, knock.
Who's there?
Sarah.
Sarah who?
Sarah cat in the house?

Knock, knock.
Who's there?
Juno.
Juno who?
Juno where the cat is?

FIRST WITCH'S CAT: What do you call an old hag who lives by the sea?
SECOND WITCH'S CAT: *A sand-witch.*

WITCH'S CAT: Are you feeling better?
WITCH: *Yes, the doctor says I can get up for a spell this afternoon.*

What kind of music did the witch's cat like best?
Hagtime.

FIRST CAT: What's your favourite meat?
SECOND CAT: *The dearest.*
FIRST CAT: And what's the dearest?
SECOND CAT: *Venison, of course.*

What kind of tree is like a cat's credit card?
Pussy willow.

JANE: Our cat died after falling into a bucket
of varnish.
WAYNE: *I bet he had a lovely finish.*

FIRST CAT: Tennis is my favourite game.
SECOND CAT: *Why?*
FIRST CAT: My two brothers are in that
racket.

What happened to the cat who liked eating sugar?
He got a lump in the throat.

A patient rushed round to his doctor, fearing he had got rabies from being bitten by a mad cat. 'Quick,' he said to the doctor, 'give me a pencil and a piece of paper!'

'Do you want to make your will?' asked the doctor.

'No, just a list of people I want to bite,' replied the man.

FIRST CAT: Do you think it's going to rain?
SECOND CAT: *That depends on the weather.*

Knock, knock.
Who's there?
Cattle.
Cattle who?
Cattle purr if you stroke it.

Knock, knock.
Who's there?
Kenneth.
Kenneth who?
Kenneth little kitten go out to play?

Which side does a cat sleep on?
Both. All of it goes to sleep at the same time.

Why didn't the shark attack the ship's cat
when it fell overboard?
Because it was a man-eating shark.

Why do tom-cats fight?
They like raising a stink.

Why did the cat scratch a hole right through
the carpet?
He wanted to see the floor show.

Why is a stupid ginger tom like a biscuit?
They're both ginger nuts.

What happened to the cat who was trampled
to death by a herd of sheep?
He was dyed in the wool.

FIRST CAT: My brother has warts.
SECOND CAT: *What are they?*
FIRST CAT: I don't know, but they have a way
of growing on you.

SALLY: My cat's a V.I.P.
WALLY: *What's a V.I.P.?*
SALLY: A Very Important Pussy.

When can a cat move as fast as a train?
When it's inside one.

As I was going to St Ives
I met a man with seven wives.
Every wife had seven sacks,
Every sack had seven cats.
Every cat had seven kits –
Kits, cats, sacks, wives:
How many were going to St Ives?

Just me – all the rest were coming *from* St
Ives!

A lady met a little boy sitting at the side of the road and crying. 'What's the matter?' she asked.

'I swapped my kitten for an ice-cream because I was hot and hungry,' sobbed the lad.

'And now you realise how much you loved him and wish you hadn't?' asked the lady.

'No. I wish I hadn't because I'm hot and hungry again!'

How can a cat get rid of a white elephant?
Put it in a jumbo sale.

MILLY: Have you seen the Catskill Mountains?
BILLY: *No, but I've seen them kill mice.*

What do cats like to read each morning?
Mewspapers.

How does a cat go down a motorway?
Mia-oww-oww-oww!

Knock, knock.
Who's there?
Guthrie.
Guthrie who?
Guthrie mice to eat here.

Did you hear about the cat who won the milk-drinking contest?
It lapped the field.

What do you get if you cross an alley cat with a canary?
A peeping tom.

JIM: Our cat is really clever.
TIM: *Why, what does it do?*
JIM: To catch mice it eats a piece of cheese and then breathes down a mousehole.

What's a cat's favourite work by Dickens?
A Tale of Two Kitties.

What's a cat's favourite Cornish town?
Mousehole.

What do cats rest their heads on when sleeping?
Caterpillars.

Why did the cat give up tap dancing?
Because he kept falling in the sink.

FIRST CAT: Say something sweet to me.
SECOND CAT: *Lemon meringue pie.*

Why did the cat paint her claws red?
So she could hide in the strawberry bed.

There was a big smelly old tom-cat called
Inn. One day Inn got lost. How was he
found?
Inn-stinked (instinct).

What happened when the cat swallowed a
20p piece?
There was money in the kitty.

POLITE CAT: Will you join me in a dish of
   fish?
SECOND CAT: *Do you think there'll be room
   for two of us?*

FIRST CAT: What's this rubbish they've given
   us to eat?
SECOND CAT: *It's bean soup.*
FIRST CAT: I don't care what it's been, what
   is it now?

Knock, knock.
Who's there?
Miaow Major.
Miaow Major who?
Miaow Major open the door, didn't I?

Knock, knock.
Who's there?
Emmett.
Emmett who?
Emmett the front door, not at the back.

Why did the bald cat throw away his keys?
Because he didn't have any locks.

What's the difference between a cat and a
flea?
*A cat can have fleas, but a flea can't have
cats.*

Why is a cat sitting on a fence like a coin?
*Because it has a head on one side and a tail
on the other.*

Why did the tabby cat paint her head yellow?
To see if blondes had more fun.

A cat wanted to cross a stream. There was no boat and no bridge, and the stream was too deep and fast-flowing to swim. How did it cross?
You give up? So did the cat!

DOLLY: We bought a cat and they said it would purr more than other cats.
MOLLY: *Why?*
DOLLY: Because it's a Purrsian cat.

What does a cat in a hot country drink?
Evaporated milk.

DARREN: Spell 'mousetrap' in three letters.
SHARON: *That's not possible.*
DARREN: Yes it is: C A T.

Knock, knock.
Who's there?
Wendy.
Wendy who?
Wendy cat comes in, I'll feed him.

Why did the cat put a lump of sugar under
his pillow at night?
So he could have sweet dreams.

FIRST CAT: Are you superstitious?
SECOND CAT: *No.*
FIRST CAT: Then lend me £13.

What happened to the cat who wore sunglasses?
He took a dim view of things.

A cat was lying in the sun and getting very hot. 'Why don't you move out of the sun if you're too hot?' asked his friend.

'Why should I?' replied the cat. 'I was here first.'

FIRST CAT: I love sunbathing.
SECOND CAT: *So do I. I could lie in the sun all day and all night.*

FIRST CAT: I think I've got sunstroke.
SECOND CAT: *Well, you basked for it.*

MAN IN PET SHOP: How can I hire a cat basket?
PET SHOP OWNER: *You could try standing it on a table.*

FIRST CAT: It's true, you know, that TV causes violence.
SECOND CAT: *What makes you say that?*
FIRST CAT: Every time young Jimmy switches on the set his Dad hits him.

FIRST CAT: I once ate a watch.
SECOND CAT: *Wasn't that time-consuming?*

Why is a cat's nose in the middle of its face?
Because it's the centre (scenter).

Why did the cat cut a hole in his umbrella?
So he could see when it had stopped raining.

What did the cat do when he'd swallowed some cheese?
Waited by the mousehole with baited breath.

Which kind of cat is useful in a library?
A catalogue.

Why is a cat longer in the morning than at night?
Because he's let out each morning and taken in each night.

71

CUSTOMER: This looks like a nice cake.
FRIEND: *It looks as if mice have been eating it.*
SHOP ASSISTANT: That's impossible. The cat's been lying on it all night.

FIRST CAT: I see you're wearing your Easter whiskers.
SECOND CAT: *Why do you call them that?*
FIRST CAT: Because they've got egg all over them.

What are the last hairs on a cat's tail called?
Cats' hairs.

VISITOR: Why is your cat staring so hard at me?
LADY OF THE HOUSE: *It's probably because you're eating off his plate.*

SUE: My cat's really clever.
PRUE: *How do you know?*
SUE: I asked him to take 50 away from 50 and he said nothing.

How can you stop cats digging up your garden?
Hide the spade.

What do you call a cat with eight legs who likes swimming?
An octopuss.

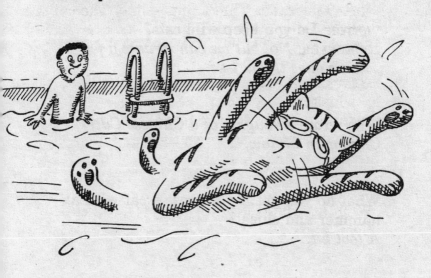

ANNE: I've lost my cat.
DAN: *Why don't you put an advertisement in the paper?*
ANNE: Don't be silly, he can't read.

NELLIE: What's your favourite animal?
KELLY: *A cat.*
NELLIE: And what's your favourite colour?
KELLY: *Purple.*
NELLIE: And what's your favourite number?
KELLY: *Five.*
NELLIE: Have you ever seen a five-legged purple cat?

DORA: Why is your cat so small?
FLORA: *He was raised on condensed milk.*

VISITOR: Do you keep wild cats?
ZOOKEEPER: *No, but we can irritate a few tame ones if you like.*

Who wrote *Thoughts of a Chinese Cat?*
Chairman Miaow.

What do you get if you cross a cat with a hammer and chisel?
A tool kit.

MARY: Yesterday my cat fell out of an 80-foot tree.
GARY: *Was it hurt?*
MARY: No, because it had only gone up three feet.

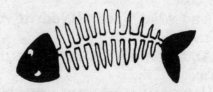

LION'S BUSY

'Sorry, lion's busy,' is what the telephonist says when you ring up and ask to speak to Lenny the lion. Here are some more jokes about the king of beasts.

What do you get if you cross a parrot with a lion?
A creature that bites off your arm and then says, 'Who's a pretty boy?'

A group of lions in a safari park were watching a coachload of tourists drive past. 'Isn't it awful', said one lion, 'to keep them caged up like that?'

What game do lions play at parties?
Swallow My Leader.

What's a lion cub's favourite toy?
A catapult.

What's a catalogue?
A lion sitting on a tree trunk.

Why should you never do sums near a lion?
Because if you add 4 and 4 you get eight.

What do you do if a lion runs away with your football?
Buy another one.

Why did the lion buy a leopard-skin coat?
He wanted to go around in disguise.

What did Tarzan say when the lion attacked him?
'Ah-ah-ah-ah-ah!' (Tarzan yell)

MR FEATHER: That's a lovely stuffed lion.
MR FLIVVER: *Yes. My great-uncle shot it when he was on safari with my grandfather.*
MR FEATHER: What's it stuffed with?
MR FLIVVER: *My grandfather.*

BEN: What's a lion's principal part?
KEN: *His mane.*

If an African lion fought an African tiger, who would win?
Neither – there's no such thing as an African tiger.

Why is it dangerous to tunnel under
Paddington Station?
Because it's a main-lion station.

Did you hear about the stupid lion who lay
down to gnaw a bone?
When he got up he only had three legs.

DAVE: Are you sure you want me to put my
    head in the lion's mouth?
DANIEL: *Yes.*
DAVE: But I thought you were my friend!

TEACHER: What's the Equator?
SILLY SUE: *An imaginary lion running round
    the Earth.*

What's a lion's favourite dance?
The fang-dango.

What's the difference between a gentle lion
and a bad scholar?
One rarely bites; the other barely writes.

Why was the lion called Ginger?
Because Ginger snaps.

What does a lion tidy its mane with?
A catacomb.

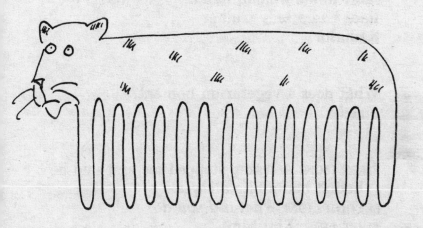

Sign in Safari Park: Trespassers may be eaten.

What goes chomp, chomp, suck, ouch!
A lion with a bad tooth.

What did the polite lion say after the dentist had checked his teeth?
'Fangs very much.'

Can a toothless lion bite you?
No, but it can give you a nasty suck!

Radi was a circus lion,
Radi was a woman hater.
Radi had a lady trainer–
Radiator.

What does a vegetarian lion eat?
Swedes.

FIRST LION: A tramp stopped me and said he
    hadn't had a bite all week.
SECOND LION: *What did you do?*
FIRST LION: I bit him.

FIRST ZOOKEEPER: We've got a new lion.
SECOND ZOOKEEPER: *Does he bite?*
FIRST ZOOKEEPER: I don't know. I want you
    to help me find out.

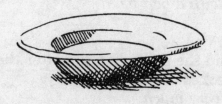

What do you get if you cross a lion with a
woodpecker?
A creature that knocks before it eats you.

Why did the lion feel sick after he'd eaten
the missionary?
Because it's hard to keep a good man down.

On which day do lions eat people?
Chewsday.

When is a lion's roar worse than its bite?
When it's been eating garlic.

What should you do with a starving lion?
Give it a hand.

81

JENNY: Can you spell 'blind lion'?
KENNY: *Yes. B-L-I-N-D L-I-O-N.*
JENNY: No, it's B-L-N-D L-O-N. If it had two "I"s it wouldn't be blind.

Have you read *Swedish Lion Cubs* by Bjorn Free?

MAN IN SAFARI PARK: A lion just bit my hand.
KEEPER: *Shall I put something on it?*
MAN: No, it'll be miles away by now.

What do you get if you cross a lion with a mouse?
Mighty Mouse!

Where does a huge lion sit at the cinema?
Anywhere it wants to!

Why don't lions shave?
Because nine out of ten cats prefer whiskers.

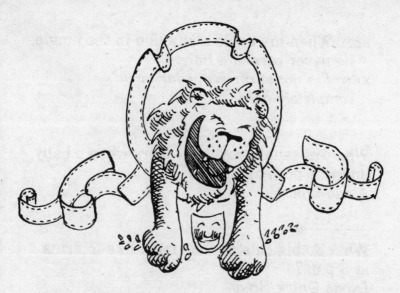

What did one lion in the zoo say to another?
'Let's be pen-pals.'

Where did the lion look for honey on the Ark?
In the Ark hives.

When is a lion not a lion?
When it turns into a cage.

LION-TAMER: You should be ashamed to give me such a poultry pay packet.
CIRCUS BOSS: *You mean 'paltry'.*
LION-TAMER: No, 'poultry' – this is chicken-feed.

BEN: When my uncle met a lion in the jungle he never turned a hair.

KEN: *I'm not surprised, your uncle's completely bald!*

Who was sent to cover the story when a baby lion was born at the zoo?
A cub reporter.

What do big cats in the jungle like to drink at 3 p.m.?
Lyons Quick Brew.

Why is a lion in the desert like Christmas?
Because it has sandy claws.

What did the two lions say when they saw some hunters in a jeep?
'Oh look, meals on wheels.'

Knock, knock.
Who's there?
Ralph.
Ralph who?
Ralph, Ralph, I'm a little lion cub.

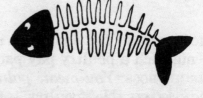

What's the difference between a
thunderstorm and a lion with toothache?
*One pours with rain; the other roars with
pain.*

What did the lion do when the man put his
head in its mouth to see how many teeth it
had?
*It closed its mouth to see how many heads
the man had.*

MRS FEATHER: If you were a good father you'd take your son to see the lions at the zoo.

MR FEATHER: *If the lions at the zoo want him they can come and get him!*

There were ten lions in the zoo. All but nine escaped. How many were left?
Nine.

What happens when a lion runs into the buffers at a railway station?
It's the end of the lion.

What do an umpire's assistant and a zookeeper have in common?
They are both lionsmen (linesmen).

A man who got lost in the jungle suddenly found himself face to face with a lion, and fainted from shock. When he came to he found the lion was saying its prayers.

'Thank you for not eating me,' sighed the man, with relief.

'Shhh,' said the lion. 'I'm saying grace.'

What happened when Ray accidentally trod on the lion's tail?
He became X-Ray.

HOLLY: In the park I was surrounded by lions.
MOLLY: *Lions? In the park?*
HOLLY: Yes, dandelions.

SUE: My father's a vet at the zoo.
PRUE: *Really? How does he treat the lions?*
SUE: With the greatest respect!

What do you get if you cross a lion with a Rottweiler?
I'm not sure, but when it barks you had better listen!

What's the best way to talk to a man-eating lion?
On the phone.

MAEVE: Have you ever seen a man-eating lion?
DAVE: *No, but I've seen a man eating rabbit.*

FIRST CLOWN: What was the name of that chap who used to work here – you know, the man who put his right arm in the lion's mouth?
SECOND CLOWN: *I can't remember, but they call him Lefty now.*

FIRST EXPLORER: If a lion were stalking you, what steps would you take?
SECOND EXPLORER: *The longest I could!*

A huge lion in the jungle met a mouse. 'You're very small,' it remarked.
'I know,' replied the mouse. 'But, you see, I've been ill.'

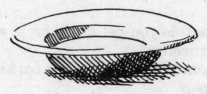

COLONEL BLIMP: I used to hunt lions in the Arctic.

COLONEL BLIMP: *But there aren't any lions in the Arctic.*

COLONEL BLIMP: I know, I shot them all.

What do you call a lion that's very particular about its appearance?
A dandy-lion.

Why was the lion-tamer towed away?
He parked on a yellow lion.

Why was the lion-tamer towed away twice?
He parked on a double yellow lion.

Knock, knock.
Who's there?
Lionel.
Lionel who?
Lionel roar if you tread on its tail.

A lion was strolling through the jungle when he met a giraffe. 'Who is the king of beasts?' he asked.

'You are, mighty lion,' replied the giraffe.

Pleased, the lion continued on his way until he met a wildebeest. 'Who is the king of beasts?' asked the lion again.

'Oh, you are, mighty lion,' replied the wildebeest.

Then the lion met an elephant, and repeated his question. The elephant didn't answer. Instead, it picked up the lion in its trunk, swung him up into the air, crashed him against a tree trunk, and finally deposited him in the middle of a very muddy watering hole.

The lion picked himself up, and crawled out, licking his wounds. 'There's no need to be so cross just because you didn't know the answer,' he said.

CHAS: Lions have a great sense of humour.
BAZ: *How do you know?*
CHAS: I told one a joke and it absolutely roared!

Who went into the lion's den and came out
alive?
Daniel.
Who went into the tiger's den and came out
alive?
The tiger!

TRACEY: Did I tell you about the time I was
face to face with a lion?
STACEY: *No, what happened?*
TRACEY: There it was, snarling, poised to
spring ...
STACEY: *What did you do?*
TRACEY: I turned round and went to see what
was in the next cage.

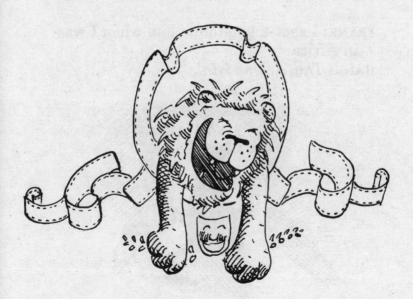

OLD KEEPER: Don't be afraid, this lion is very gentle. He'll eat off your hand.
NEW KEEPER: *That's what I'm afraid of!*

What do you get if you cross a lion with a footballer?
I don't know, but when it tries to score a goal no one stops it.

Knock, knock.
Who's there?
Aurora.
Aurora who?
Aurora's what a lion is.

FRANK: I shot a two-tonne lion when I was in Africa.
HANK: *That's some lyin'.*

A man was walking through the streets with a lion on a lead. A policeman approached him and said, 'You should take that lion to the zoo.'

'Right,' said the man. 'I'll do that.'

The next day the policeman was surprised to see the same man again, still with the lion on a lead. 'I thought I told you to take that animal to the zoo,' he said.

'I did,' replied the man. 'And he enjoyed it so much I'm taking him to the cinema today.'

FIRST CIRCUS PERFORMER: Aren't you afraid to put your head in the lion's mouth?
SECOND CIRCUS PERFORMER: *Yes. I'm afraid of the dark.*

Have you read *Lion Taming* by Claudia Arms?

BERYL: There I was, wild horses prancing about, lions in front of me and behind me. . . .
CHERYL: *And then what?*
BERYL: And then the roundabout stopped.

REG IT, REG IT

Why was the tiger called Reg It?
Because it went everywhere backwards, of
course! All the jokes in this section are
about tigers, both forwards and backwards.
After all, they're just great big tabby cats,
aren't they?

What did the idiot call his pet tiger?
Spot.

Why should you never grab a tiger by its
tail?
*It may be the tail of the tiger, but it could be
the end of you!*

Knock, knock.
Who's there?
Omar.
Omar who?
Omar goodness, there's a great big tiger
right behind you!

What do you call a Siberian tiger?
A cool cat.

COLONEL BLIMP: In India, people chased
tigers on horseback.
COLONEL BLUMP: *Amazing! I didn't know
tigers could ride horses!*

COLONEL FLIMP: I say, you just shot my wife!
COLONEL FLUMP: *I'm frightfully sorry, old
bean, here, have a shot at mine!*

COLONEL GLIMP: Let's go home, we haven't
bagged a single tiger all day.
COLONEL GLUMP: *Let's miss a couple more
before we go.*

COLONEL LIMP: I've just seen a huge tiger!
COLONEL LUMP: *Did you let him have both
barrels?*
COLONEL LIMP: Both barrels? I let him have
the whole gun!

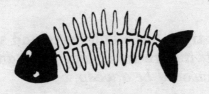

MRS SHUFFLEBOTTOM: We went on holiday to shoot tigers.
MRS SIDEBOTTOM: *Any luck?*
MRS SHUFFLEBOTTOM: Yes. We didn't meet any.

A hunter was showing off his trophies, including his tiger-skin rug. His guest didn't like to see a tiger reduced to being a rug, and said so.

'It was either him or me,' explained the hunter.

'Well, I suppose he makes a better rug than you would,' sighed his guest.

What's a hunter's motto?
Never pat a tiger until it's a rug.

What's the difference between a lion and a tiger?
A tiger has the mane part missing.

What flies from flower to flower and can bite off your head?
A tiger moth.

Why is a tiger large and fierce and striped?
Because if it were small and fierce and striped it would be a wasp.

What flower has a deadly bite?
A tiger lily.

What do you get if you cross a zebra with a tiger?
Stripes before the eyes.

What do you get if you cross fifty stars with a tiger?
The American flag.

How does a tiger get its stripes?
From sunbathing behind bars.

What do you get if you cross a pig with a tiger?
Striped sausages and streaky bacon.

If a tiger loses its tail, where can it get another?
At a re-tail store.

A man was applying for a job at the zoo. The advertisement had said the applicant must be fit, and not accident-prone, and when the man turned up for his interview with his arm swathed in bandages, the interviewer asked, 'What happened to your arm? Did you have an accident?'

'A tiger bit me,' replied the man.

'Wasn't that an accident?' asked the interviewer.

'Certainly not,' said the man. 'That mean-tempered old brute did it on purpose.'

FIRST THE GOOD NEWS: I got a tiger for
  Christmas.
NOW THE BAD NEWS: I get the cage next
  Christmas.

How did the sabre-toothed tiger pass his
exams?
With extinction.

What did the elephant say when it saw a
tiger walking through long grass?
'Now you see him, now you don't.'

What's worse than raining cats and dogs?
Raining lions and tigers.

What's a definition of a tiger?
A lion behind bars.

What's striped and bounces?
A tiger on a pogo stick.

What's brown and yellow, brown and yellow,
brown and yellow?
A tiger rolling down a hill.

TEACHER: Who wrote the American national anthem?
CLEVER DICK: *Tarzan and his tiger friend.*
TEACHER: What do you mean?
CLEVER DICK: *Well, it's called 'Tarzan Stripes Forever', isn't it?*

How can you get a set of teeth put in for free?
Hit a tiger.

Did the people like the tigers at the safari park?
Yes, they were a howling success.

There was a young lady of Riga
Who smiled as she rode on a tiger.
They returned from the ride
With the lady inside
And the smile on the face of the tiger.

What do you get if you cross a plum with a man-eating tiger?
A purple people eater.

When is a man-eating tiger likely to come into the house?
When the door is open.

What's it called when you're eaten by a tiger?
A catastrophe.

FIRST TIGER: I don't feel well.
SECOND TIGER: *It must be someone you ate.*

Knock, knock.
Who's there?
Armageddon.
Armageddon who?
Armageddon out of this place, it's full of man-eating tigers!

SPOTS BEFORE THE EYES

If the idiot called his pet tiger Spot, did his friend call her pet cheetah Stripe? We shall never know, but here are lots of jokes about large, fierce spotted cats.

A man had a pet cheetah who could play the violin. 'Is it true', asked his friend, 'that it learned to play in six easy lessons?'

'Yes,' replied the man. 'It was the next 600 that were the difficult ones.'

Where might you find a cheetah?
That depends where you leave him.

Advertisement in the Daily Mews: For sale, pet cheetah. Gentle, clean, and will eat anything. Especially fond of children.

Why can't you trust an Indian leopard?
Because it's a cheetah.

Can a leopard change its spots?
Well, when it gets tired of one spot it can move to another.

Two friends were on safari in the jungle. Said the first, 'I've just spotted a leopard.'
   'Don't be silly,' said his friend. 'They're born that way.'

Did you hear about the leopard who took six baths a day?
He was so clean he was spotless.

What's yellow and black with red spots?
A leopard with measles.

A man was telling his friend how his wife wanted a car for her birthday. 'She likes old cars,' he said, 'and would like a Jaguar.'

A few weeks later the friends met again. 'Did you buy your wife the Jaguar?' asked one.

'Yes,' replied the man. 'But she'd only had it a week when it ate her.'

What do you get if you cross a man-eating leopard with a dog?
An animal that eats people and then buries their bones.

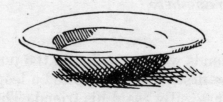

What do you call a cheetah's relatives?
Catkin.

A man was walking down the road with a cheetah on a lead. Another man called across to him, 'Where on earth did you get him from?'

'I won him in a raffle,' answered the cheetah.

Why couldn't the leopard escape from the zoo?
Because he was always spotted.

MRS GREEN: Where did you get that leopard skin?
MRS BROWN: *We went hunting with a club.*
MRS GREEN: Wasn't that dangerous, hunting leopards with a club?
MRS BROWN: *Oh no. Lots of the club's members had guns.*

Harry's Uncle Wilmot suffered from indigestion and a bad temper. One day Harry told his friend Henry that Uncle Wilmot had disappeared while on safari.

'Oh dear,' said Henry, 'what happened to him?'

'I think', said Harry, 'that something he disagreed with ate him.'

'Quick!' shouted the hunter. 'Shoot that leopard on the spot! He's dangerous!'

'Don't be daft,' called his friend. 'Which spot?'

Have you read *The Panther's Escape* by Gay Topen?

What do you call a cat
who strolls round the
jungle in a leather
suit with a safety
pin through its ear?
*The Punk
Panther.*

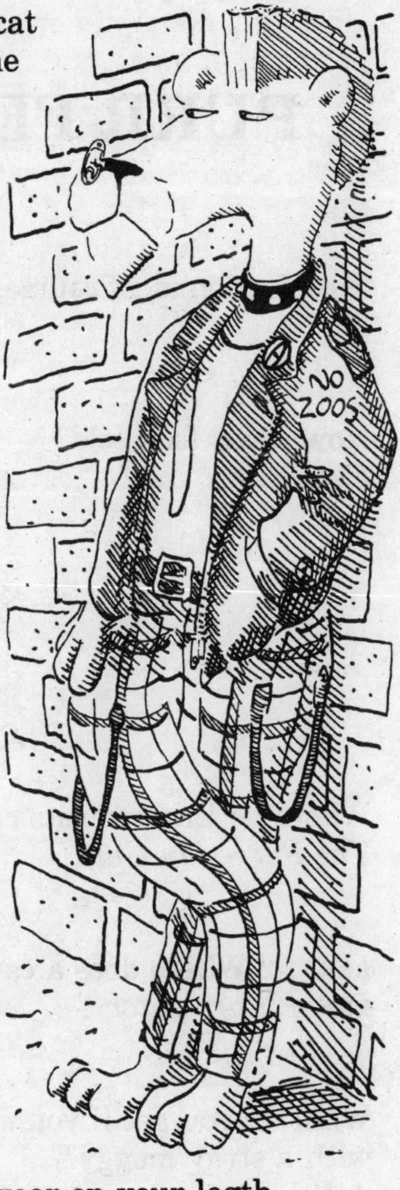

What did the
Pink Panther say
when he stepped
on the ant?
'Dead-ant,
dead-ant, dead-ant,
dead-ant,
dead-ant . . .'
(to Pink Panther
tune).

What does a Pink
Panther do?
Makes pink panths.

Knock, knock.
Who's there?
Panther.
Panther who?
Panther what you wear on your legth.

PURR-FECTION

Purr-fection is, of course, what all cats strive for.

How is cat food sold?
Purr can.

Where do Eastern cats come from?
The Purr-sian Gulf.

BERNIE: Where does a cat go when it's dead?
ERNIE: *Purr-gatory?*

What do you get if you cross a Chinese cat with a stray moggy?
A Peking tom.

'Doctor, doctor, my cat has swallowed a whole bottle of aspirins. What shall I do?'
'Try to give him an extra-large headache.'

A lady called her cat Trouble. One night when he hadn't come home, she put on her dressing-gown and slippers, and picked up the poker in case she met anyone nasty, and went out to prowl around the streets looking for him. A policeman spotted her.

"Ello, 'ello, 'ello, what are you up to, eh?' he asked.

The lady frowned at him. 'I'm looking for Trouble,' she said.

Knock, knock.
Who's there?
Arthur.
Arthur who?
Arthur any more kittens in that basket?

Knock, knock.
Who's there?
Felix.
Felix who?
Felix his bottom again, I'll scream!

How can you get six cats in a matchbox?
Take the matches out first.

FIRST CAT: You're not looking too good.
SECOND CAT: *No, I'm not feeling up to scratch.*

What's the definition of a cat?
An animal that never cries over spilt milk.

A lady went into a shop to buy some quilted material to make a snug sleeping-bag for her cat.

'How much do you want?' asked the shop assistant.

'I don't know,' replied the lady.

'Well, why don't you measure your cat's present bed?'

'Oh, I couldn't do that. The new one's meant to be a surprise for his birthday.'

Knock, knock.
Who's there?
Puss.
Puss who?
Puss your bike if you have a puncture.

Two cats met. 'Miaow,' said the first.

'Bow, wow,' replied the second.

'What do you mean, "bow, wow"?' asked the first.

'Oh,' said the second, 'I'm learning a foreign language.'

Who was the famous cat composer?
Pussini.

What happened when an African cat escaped from the zoo?
It made headlions.

MR CRUMP: You'll never teach that cat to obey you.

MRS CRUMP: *Nonsense. Don't you remember how stubborn you were when we were first married?*

MRS CRIMP: She calls her husband and the cat by the same pet name.

MRS CRAMP: *Isn't that confusing?*

MRS CRIMP: Not really. She always speaks nicely to the cat.

TEACHER: This essay on 'My Cat' is exactly the same as your sister's, Emma.

EMMA: *Well, it's the same cat, Miss.*

Little Freddie ran into the kitchen and said to his mum, 'Mum, there's a cat as big as a tiger in the garden!'

'Nonsense, Freddie,' replied his mother. 'How many millions of times have I told you not to exaggerate?'

BILLY: My cat keeps bumping into things.

MILLY: *I thought she didn't look too good.*

MOTHER: Don't bring that stray cat into the house. It's full of fleas.

SUSIE: *Now, Tiddles, don't go into the house. It's full of fleas.*

BEN: That stray cat's very suspicious.

KEN: *Yes. Both his eyes watch each other all the time.*

How many tom-cats does it take to make a
big stinker?
A phew.

FIRST CAT: I used to hunt with thousands
under me.
SECOND CAT: *Really? Where?*
FIRST CAT: In the cemetery.

TIM: Did you ever see a fox trot?
JIM: *No, but I've seen a cat nap.*

FIRST CAT: What's worse than being with a fool?
SECOND CAT: *Fooling with a bee.*

What does a cat get if it eats foam?
Soft in the head.

'It's so hot out there the cats are taking turns to sit in each other's shadows.'

MABEL: Can a cat jump higher than a house?
MINNIE: *No.*
MABEL: Yes it can. A house can't jump.

NEIL: Did you hear about the flea circus being ruined?
NIGEL: *No, what happened?*
NEIL: A cat came along and stole the show.

How do you fatten a thin cat?
Throw him over a cliff and he'll come down 'plump'.

OWNER: My cat's hair keeps falling out. Can you give me anything to keep it in?
VET: *How about a paper bag?*

Knock, knock.
Who's there?
Avon.
Avon who?
Avon to come in the cat flap.

FIRST CAT: That old tom-cat over there is the ugliest brute I've ever seen.
SECOND CAT: *Do you mind – he's my husband.*
FIRST CAT: Oh dear, I'm so sorry.
SECOND CAT: *You're sorry! How do you think I feel?*

What do you get if you cross a cat with a kangaroo?
A pocket with nine lives.

What do you get if you cross a cat with Father Christmas?
Santa Claws.

JANE: Why does your cat go around with his mouth open?

WAYNE: *He's so lazy, it saves him having to open it each time he yawns.*

MRS GREEN: Our house is so small the mice have to stoop.

MRS BROWN: *Our house is so damp the cats catch fish!*

FIRST CAT: Why do you enjoy being stroked so much?

SECOND CAT: *I like to feel kneaded.*

Why does a large cat eat less than a small cat?

He makes a little go a long way.

FIRST CAT: Did you hear that loud noise this morning?

SECOND CAT: *Yes, was it the crack of dawn?*

FIRST CAT: No, the break of day.

What do you call a cat who's always digging in the flowerbed?
Pete (peat).

NELL: I know a cat worth £250.
DEL: *Gosh, how could a cat save so much money?*

CAT: This milk is very watery.
OWNER: *The cow must have got caught in the rain.*

What overpowers a cat without hurting it?
Sleep.

Knock, knock.
Who's there?
Owen.
Owen who?
Owen you going to let the cat in?

Knock, knock.
Who's there?
Ali.
Ali who?
Ali-luyah, you've opened the door at last!

Which animals need oiling?
Mice, because they squeak.

News headline: Local man takes first prize in cat show.

A man was going down the road with a cat in his arms. Another man called across the road, 'Where are you going with that pig?'

'It's not a pig, it's a cat!'

'Quiet, you,' shouted the man rudely. 'I wasn't talking to you, I was talking to the cat!'

How can you tell when a mummified cat is angry?
He flips his lid.

Knock, knock.
Who's there?
Lionel.
Lionel who?
Lionel get you nowhere, better tell the truth!

What has a cat's bottom at its top?
Its hindleg.

Why might a cat put the letter M in the fridge?
Because it turns ice into mice.

Why do mummified cats tell no secrets?
Because they keep everything under wraps.

CONNIE: Have you ever seen a cat make a henhouse?
DONNIE: *No, but I've seen a fox make a chicken run!*

Knock, knock.
Who's there?
Emma.
Emma who?
Emma pig when it comes to fish.

LIL: I've just bought a tom-cat.
PHIL: *Where will you keep it?*
LIL: Under the bed.
PHIL: *But what about the smell?*
LIL: He'll just have to get used to it.

A concert pianist used to practise the piano each day, and did not wish to be disturbed. One day, while he was practising, someone called to see him. Acting on instructions, the housekeeper said he was out.

'But I heard him playing!' said the caller.

'No, sir,' replied the housekeeper. 'That was just the cat walking up and down on the piano keys.'

Little Susie was sitting in front of the fire stroking her new kitten, which was purring.

'Mummy, come quickly!' shouted Susie. 'The kitten's started to boil!'

120

A man was complaining about his flat-mate, who, he said, kept pigs in the kitchen.

'The smell's terrible,' he moaned.

'Couldn't you open the window?' suggested his friend.

'What, and let out all my cats!' exclaimed the man.

What yard has four feet in it?
One containing a cat.

What do you call a woman with a cat on her head?
Kitty.

TEACHER: Who can name four members of the cat family?
MANDY: *I can, Miss – mother cat, father cat and two kittens.*

What sort of clothes does a pet cat wear?
Petticoats.

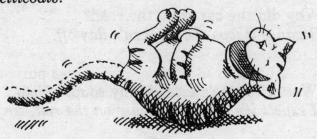

121

What's the difference between a hungry cat
and a greedy cat?
One longs to eat, the other eats too long.
What else?
With some cats it's very difficult to tell!

Knock, knock.
Who's there?
Violet.
Violet who?
Violet the cat out of the bag.

FIRST CAT: How's your nose?
SECOND CAT: *Shut up.*
FIRST CAT: So's mine – must be the weather.

OWNER: Have you anything to cure fleas on
my cat?
VET: *Possibly. What's wrong with the fleas?*

Why did the cat cross the road?
Because it was the chicken's day off.

'Waiter! There's a cat in my soup!'
'I expect it's after the mouse on the roll, sir.'

Why do Eskimo cats eat whalemeat and blubber?
Well, wouldn't you blubber if you had to eat whalemeat?

LEO: A cat must have three tails.
THEO: *Don't be silly, it hasn't.*
LEO: Yes it has. Listen. Any cat has more tails than no cat. Right?
THEO: *Yes.*
LEO: And no cat has two tails – right?
THEO: *Yes.*
LEO: Therefore any cat must have three tails!

HARRY: What was the name of that pantomime we went to? You know, the one about the cat in the chemist's shop?
LARRY: *Oh, you mean* Puss in Boots?

What do you call a cat that rushes about carrying bandages and antiseptic?
A first-aid kit.

CUSTOMER: Do you sell cats' meat?
BUTCHER: *Only if they're accompanied by a human being, madam.*

Knock, knock.
Who's there?
Ken.
Ken who?
Ken you open the door and let me in?

FIRST CAT: I hear you came from Switzerland.
SECOND CAT: *Yes.*
FIRST CAT: Was the scenery nice?
SECOND CAT: *I don't know. I could never see it, the mountains got in the way!*

FIRST CAT: I'm so unlucky my owner couldn't open my tin of food.

SECOND CAT: *I'm so unlucky the fish in my bowl swam away.*

Knock, knock.
Who's there?
Yvonne.
Yvonne who?
Yvonne lots and lots of pussy cats!